The Roadrunner

by James W. Cornett

D0444610

Cover Photograph:
Face of the Greater Roadrunner
Death Valley National Park, California

Title Page Photograph:
Roadrunner Parent Feeding Lizard To Its Young
Mojave National Preserve, California

The author offers his thanks to Sandra Vehrencamp of the Cornell
Laboratory of Ornithology, Cameron Barrows of The Center For
Natural Lands Management, and Kurt Leuschner of College of The
Desert for reviewing the manuscript for technical accuracy. Appreciation
is also extended to Jan Belknap, Clifford Neff, and my wife, Terry
Cornett, for their review of the final draft of this publication.

Unless otherwise noted, photographs are by the author.

Copyright 2001 by James W. Cornett
All rights reserved.

Published by
nature trails press
P.O. Box 846
Palm Springs, California 92263
Telephone (760) 320-2664
Fax (760) 320-6182

No part of this book may be reproduced by any means,
or transmitted or translated into a machine language
without the written permission of the author.

International Standard Book Number (ISBN): 0-937794-32-5

Contents

A Most Popular Bird

The roadrunner is unquestionably the best-known bird in the Southwest—and why not? Compared with other American birds the roadrunner is decidedly unique. It prefers to run rather than fly. It possesses an unusual appetite—an appetite that includes dangerous creatures such as rattlesnakes, scorpions, and black widow spiders. Along with a strange diet, the roadrunner has an endless assortment of vocalizations and postures that give it communication skills unmatched by most other birds. Roadrunner behavior seems odd, even comical as it wags its tail, erects its head crest and clatters its mandibles together. No wonder so many Southwestern residents have befriended this bird even enticing it into their homes for a morsel of food.

With such an engaging image, it should come as no surprise that the roadrunner is often used to promote business enterprises. More than five hundred American businesses use *roadrunner* in their name, or the bird's image in their logo. Roadrunner Courier Service in New York, Roadrunner High Speed Internet Service in Washington D.C., Roadrunner Realty in Phoenix and Roadrunner Locksmith in San Diego are but a few examples.

My interest in roadrunners began as a boy growing up in Southern California. I was, in truth, more curious about snakes than roadrunners. But many of the reptile books I found at the library described the roadrunner as the "great snake killer." I was amazed to discover that snakes of all kinds were killed and devoured, including dangerous rattlesnakes.

My family's home was in a suburb near Los Angeles and roadrunners did not occur in the immediate neighborhood. Only on those infrequent occasions when friends and I would sneak away to the outskirts of town did we see one. As the name suggests, most of the time we would glimpse a roadrunner as it ran across the road in front of us.

It was on family driving vacations that I would most often see a roadrunner, or at least its image. Together with my older brother and sister, we often coerced my parents into stopping at roadside snack stands. Inevitably, there would be an associated curio shop. Inside were depictions of roadrunners adorning all manner of souvenirs including postcards, place mats, T-shirts, porcelain statues, and coffee mugs. I once cajoled my father into letting me buy a small pocketknife imprinted with a roadrunner. Decades have passed since those family vacations, but the roadrunner image still pervades the merchandise in highway souvenir shops.

One of the most memorable recollections of the roadrunner was the cartoon series created by Chuck Jones and distributed by Warner Brothers studios. On motion picture and television screens I and millions of other children were entertained by the antics of the star *Roadrunner* character as he cleverly avoided becoming *Wile E. Coyote's* next meal. I was later to learn that the cartoon likeness bore faint resemblance to a real roadrunner and that the coyote rarely, if ever, preyed upon this bird.

As an adult, I have often been surprised to learn that visitors from the eastern United States often only know the roadrunner as the cartoon character. Frequently I hear the exclamation "So there really is a roadrunner!" In the last few decades it seems the cartoon, more than anything else, is what has made this bird so famous.

Greater Roadrunner bringing a whiptail lizard
(Cnemidophorus tigris) *to its young;*
Saguaro National Park, Arizona.

An adult Greater Roadrunner, showing the colored featherless "postorbital patch" behind the eye.

A Roadrunner Mystery

After graduating from college, I went to work at the Desert Museum in downtown Palm Springs, a city located in the Sonoran Desert of California. In my first few years I led weekly nature hikes and had much contact with the public. I fielded all kinds of questions about the desert and its plants and animals. However, there was one particular question that kept arising and for which I had no answer. "Where do the roadrunners go in winter?"

Many homeowners in rural and semi-rural regions of the Southwest regularly feed neighborhood roadrunners. Hamburger balls are the usual offering and are relished by the birds. (Feeding roadrunners hamburger should be discouraged. A nestling roadrunner given this meat by its parents is likely to develop bone deformities, partially as a result of a calcium deficiency. Instead, feed roadrunners soft cat food as it has all the nutrients necessary for proper development.) So accustomed are some of these birds to receiving handouts that on many occasions I have seen them tap on glass windows or doors with their beaks. Apparently, *they* have conditioned some homeowners to feed them through use of this glass-tapping stimulus!

Roadrunner watchers usually know individual birds that traverse their neighborhood. They correctly predict the time of arrival, nuances in behavior and peculiar aspects about the appearance of each bird. Although male and female roadrunners cannot be distinguished by appearance, individual birds often have distinctive visual characteristics: a toe without a nail, a drooping wing or, most often, something less than a perfect bill. The bill tip may be broken off, the two mandibles may not fit perfectly together, or a small piece may be missing from an edge. Homeowners know when a specific roadrunner is no longer coming to visit them because of these distinguishing features.

In dozens of instances I have heard desert residents relate how a particular roadrunner visited them daily through the spring, summer and fall. Then suddenly in early winter the bird's daily appearance stopped. Sometimes the roadrunner just became less consistent in its visits; more often, it disappeared for weeks, or even months. In spring the bird would return and resume daily visitation. The cycle might be repeated over several years. My own personal observations have been similar to the experience of desert residents. A review of field notes clearly shows a precipitous drop in roadrunner observations during winter.

Does something mysterious happen to roadrunners during the winter season? Do they move to more favorable habitats or migrate to more southerly latitudes? Are old or very young birds unable to survive the cold winter months? These and many other questions aroused my curiosity and sent me on a decade-long investigation into the behavior and ecology of this highly unusual bird. Hopefully, an answer to the roadrunner's winter disappearance may soon be forthcoming.

A roadrunner uses its wings to distract a striking
snake in Organ Pipe Cactus National Monument.

A roadrunner forages along
a Desert Willow-lined wash at the Living
Desert, Palm Desert, California.

The Greater Roadrunner can reach a top speed of nearly twenty miles per hour–
not particularly fast even by human standards. It can, however, accelerate to this
speed much more rapidly than any human. Its maneuverability and, albeit
limited, power of flight make it an elusive creature.

Resident or Visitor?

Many birds migrate from Mexico to the American Southwest in springtime. Once in the United States they breed, lay eggs, and raise their young. In late summer and fall, these same birds return to Mexico, and elsewhere in the subtropics, where they spend the winter. Hooded orioles, white-winged doves, and ash-throated flycatchers are but three examples of strong flyers that follow this migratory pattern. All of these species become rare or disappear entirely from the American Southwest in winter due to their southward migratory flights.

By contrast, roadrunners do not have the capability of flying even a hundred yards let alone migrating hundreds of miles into Mexico. A roadrunner can flap its wings for twenty or thirty yards if vigorously pursued. Rarely, however, does it reach even ten feet off the ground and the last half of a flight is usually a glide. If some strangely curious person were to drop a roadrunner from a plane at an altitude of five thousand feet, its diminutive wing muscles could not sustain a glide much less active flight. In such a scenario the bird would soon plummet to the earth like a stone. Flights normally occur only when the roadrunner must escape an enemy or reach a perch. Migratory flights are just not possible for the roadrunner.

Roadrunners are almost exclusively terrestrial birds that derive their mobility from powerful legs and exceptional running ability. They have been clocked at speeds of nearly twenty miles per hour. This is not as fast as human sprinters (24 m.p.h.) or racehorses (38 m.p.h.), but roadrunners can attain top speeds much faster than humans or horses. The fanning of their wings and tail also enable to them to break rapidly and turn on a dime, perhaps with more maneuverability than any other terrestrial animal in America.

Run as they might, the available evidence indicates that roadrunners are strictly resident birds that remain in the same general area for life. A pair I observed near my home in the Sonoran Desert of southeastern California remained together for at least three years. Biologists Leon Folse and Keith Arnold (1978), studying roadrunners in south Texas, placed leg bands on three pairs and found that they stayed together in the same immediate area for at least two years. Another of Folse and Arnold's banded individuals was recaptured just two hundred meters from where it had been captured five years before. This data, and a great deal of anecdotal evidence, strongly suggest that roadrunners are not migratory but are lifetime occupants of their territory.

The roadrunner uses its powerful legs to launch itself into the air. Two or three wing beats are usually sufficient for it to reach an elevated perch. The roadrunner returns to the ground by hopping off its perch and gliding to the earth.

Adult Greater Roadrunner on alert in Death Valley National Park.

What Is A Roadrunner?

Many visitors to the Southwest have no idea what a roadrunner is. For the record, the roadrunner is a bird and, as such, possesses all the features associated with this class of vertebrates: a body covered with feathers, feet covered with scales, a beak with no teeth and wings. Obvious in fact, but not in casual observation, is the egg-laying habit of the female. All of these characteristics are shared with members of what biologists call the Class Aves, or to what we normally refer to as *birds*.

Further examination of the roadrunner reveals certain features not shared by all members of the Class Aves. In the American Southwest, roadrunner feet and the impressions they make on soft sand are unique. The roadrunner leaves a single-file line of X-shaped tracks that can be confused with little else. These tracks reveal a condition referred to as zygodactylous feet. This anatomical trait of the roadrunner is found in only a few avian groups including parrots, toucans, woodpeckers and cuckoos. It is the latter group, the cuckoos, to which the roadrunner belongs. All members of each of these four bird groups are zygodactyl meaning the two outer toes point backwards and the second and third toes point forward. (Most birds have three toes pointing forward and one backward.) Since the roadrunner is the only terrestrial species in America with this X-shaped toe pattern, its tracks are easy to identify.

Members of the roadrunner's family, the bird family Cuculidae or cuckoos, are distinguished in having long tails and upper mandibles that are arched (only slightly in the case of the roadrunner). These two characteristics visually separate cuckoos from woodpeckers, the only other zygodactyl group found in America.

Typical roadrunner "X" shaped tracks;
Big Bend National Park, Texas.

17

A Greater Roadrunner captures a hatchling common whipsnake.

The Cuckoo Family contains 136 species distributed on all continents except Antarctica. Three of these species occur in the American Southwest. Besides the roadrunner there is the much smaller Yellow-billed Cuckoo, *Coccyzus americanus*, that can be found nesting along tree-lined streams and river courses; and an occasional visitor from Mexico known as the Groove-billed Ani, *Crotophaga sulcirostris*.

The roadrunner of the American Southwest belongs to the genus *Geococcyx* (pronounced gee-oh-kok'-siks). *Geo* is of Greek origin and refers to the earth. In combination with other words it literally means "of the earth." *Coccy* is also a Greek root and refers to any species of bird belonging to the Cuckoo Family. Translated into English *Geococcyx* means "cuckoo of the earth" or "ground dwelling cuckoo."

There is a combination of features that distinguish *Geococcyx* from other genera in the Cuckoo Family. Most noticeable is the feather head crest. When the roadrunner is aroused and the crest is raised, it effectively doubles the vertical dimension of the head. The white, orange, and blue featherless skin behind each eye (known as the postorbital patch) is also characteristic of the genus. Additionally, *Geococcyx* has a heavy charcoal-colored beak, short rounded wings, long neck, and long powerful legs for running. The lengthy tail, though a very noticeable feature, is not unique to the genus and in fact is typical among members of the Cuckoo Family. Most first-time observers of a roadrunner also judge it to be a rather large bird. There are, however, several other terrestrial cuckoos living in the New World tropics that are larger than the American roadrunner.

There is not one, but two species in the genus *Geococcyx* and so there are actually two kinds of roadrunner. The roadrunner occurring in the United States is the larger of the two and has been designated as the Greater Roadrunner with the scientific name *Geococcyx californianus*. The second half of the Greater Roadrunner's scientific name, *californianus*, reflects the state from which the first collected specimen was described in the scientific literature.

A roadrunner preening the base of its tail feathers
with its bill in Red Rock Canyon National Recreation Area, Nevada.

Lesser Roadrunner, Geococcyx velox. *Photograph by Rick Bowers.*

The other roadrunner is one-third smaller and appropriately named the Lesser Roadrunner with the technical name of *Geococcyx velox*. *Velox* is a form of veloc which in Latin means swift or speedy. The Lesser Roadrunner has habits that are similar to those of the Greater Roadrunner but its range is further south in central Mexico and Central America. Apparently, the only area where the ranges of these two birds overlap is in extreme southeastern Sonora, Mexico (Russell and Monson, 1998). In addition to the size difference, the two members of the genus *Geococcyx* can be distinguished from each other by the color of the postorbital patch. In the Greater Roadrunner the skin directly behind the eye is white grading to orange with blue on the top and on the bottom of the patch. In the Lesser Roadrunner the bare skin directly behind the eye is completely blue not white.

Although roadrunners roost and nest in shrubs and trees, compared with most birds they are a bit clumsy as they move among the branches. Photograph taken in Anza-Borrego Desert State Park, California.

Roadrunner Distribution

Greater Roadrunner

Lesser Roadrunner

Finding A Roadrunner

The Greater Roadrunner is essentially a bird of arid and semiarid lands in the American Southwest and northern Mexico. It reaches its greatest densities in open country where meager rainfall only supports shrublands or shortgrass prairies. Occasional trees or arborescent cacti, however, must be present to provide sites for roadrunner nests. The map to the left shows the distribution of the Greater Roadrunner in the United States and Mexico, the only two countries in which this bird occurs. The distribution of the Lesser Roadrunner is shown in black.

Within its range the Greater Roadrunner occupies a surprising variety of habitats. Alluvial plains and flatlands are favored but hills and broad canyonlands are also occupied. Roadrunner tracks are often seen on hummocks and dunes, clearly indicating the birds live in sandy habitats as well. Roadrunners occurr in coastal scrublands along Southern California's Pacific Coast, in yucca forests in Nevada, pine and magnolia lands in eastern Texas, and at the bottom of the Grand Canyon. Roadrunners are seen below sea level in the Mojave Desert's Death Valley and there is a very unusual record of a roadrunner having been observed at an elevation of 9,500 feet in the mountains of New Mexico (Bailey, 1928).

Roadrunners are not, however, found everywhere within their range. Over vast areas of the desert Southwest they are completely absent. This is generally **not** because there is insufficient food. Rather it is because there are no suitable nesting and roosting sites. Large or dense cacti, shrubs and trees are important to roadrunners because they provide shade and reduce the need for evaporative cooling during the hot summer months. These plant forms provide insulation from winter cold as well. Large, dense plants also provide protection from predators at night when roadrunners are sleeping and most vulnerable. Finally, shrubs and trees, particularly branching cholla cacti, dissuade predators such as hawks, large snakes, and foxes from approaching a roadrunner nest and devouring the young. All of these factors are important, but the protection afforded the eggs and young is probably the most critical.

Surprisingly, the optimal conditions for roadrunners apparently exist around the margins of retirement communities in the southwestern United States. In such areas these birds have the best of all worlds. Open flatlands exist where they can hunt traditional foods of insects and lizards. They also have large trees and shrubs of residential neighborhoods for roosting and nesting. Residential areas also provide drinking water and unique food resources such as crickets, cockroaches, snails, black widows, nestling birds, house mice, and occasional handouts from human residents. (See Charlene Webster, 2000, for details of roadrunners in urban environments.)

Perhaps most important is what retirement communities do **not** have—children and free-ranging cats. Children often harass and disturb the local wildlife by giving chase, throwing rocks, or trying to capture small animals. (I know, I was a child with a slingshot who, for a time, threatened the well-being of many birds and small animals in my neighborhood.)

Even more threatening to roadrunners are pet cats that are allowed to roam through residential developments. One cat can exterminate, or at least drive away, any roadrunner that might otherwise take up residence in an area. Residents of retirement communities generally do not have domestic cats since they often leave for extended periods to visit family members, travel, or vacate

Roadrunner habitat in Anza-Borrego Desert State Park, California.

the Southwest during the hot summer months. Fortunately for road-runners, domestic cats don't fit well into such a life-style.

In the midwestern United States, many tall grass prairies and for-ests have been converted to agricultural use, homesites, and golf courses. This kind of land clearing, with a possible change in climate towards increasing aridity, has inadvertently created additional habitat for the roadrunner. Consequently, in the last few decades, the Greater Roadrunner has expanded its distribution to include southern Kansas (Thompson and Ely, 1989), south-central Arkansas (James and Neal, 1986), western Louisiana (Lowery, 1976), and southwestern Missouri (Robbins and Easterla, 1992). This trend may continue as more wild lands are opened up due to the pressure of an expanding human population.

Greater Roadrunner habitat in the Chihuahuan Desert of western Texas.

Roadrunners roost and nest in palo verde trees that line washes in Organ Pipe Cactus National Monument, Arizona.

In Search of Food

If the old adage is true that *you are what you eat* then the roadrunner is all things. It eats just about any animal that can be swallowed whole as well as many types of seeds and fruits. In fact, it may very well have the most diverse diet of any bird in America. This factor contributes both to the roadrunner's success and notoriety.

In 1916 Harold Bryant of the University of California wrote the first, and still the most comprehensive, study on the diet of the roadrunner. He collected data by hiring employees of the Department of Fish and Game to shoot roadrunners so that he could examine the contents of their stomachs. Over a two-year period eighty-four roadrunners were taken in the course of the research.

By today's standards Bryant's approach might seem barbaric. But scientific methods were different in the early 1900s and such procedures were commonplace. What's more, Bryant was trying to save the birds. At the time, it was believed that roadrunners were ravenous predators of quail and were depleting the numbers of these popular game birds. Roadrunners were seen, like many other predators, as creatures to be shot on site for the benefit of useful species. Because of this persecution, ornithologists were witnessing the disappearance of roadrunners from large areas of the state.

After two years of research, Bryant found that roadrunners in Southern California rarely captured and consumed birds of any kind. Not a single quail was found in the digestive tract of any roadrunner in the study. This was not to say that roadrunners did not eat quail. Bryant was the first to admit that roadrunners did occasionally capture and consume many kinds of small birds. As he noted in his report, there had been many eyewitness accounts of predation on hatchling quail. What Bryant's research demonstrated, however, was that roadrunners were not important predators of these game birds. In my own observations, I have often observed roadrunners attempt to capture baby quail but have never seen one succeed. Typically, a male and female quail with young become

A roadrunner has captured and killed a
desert iguana, Dipsosaurus dorsalis.

very aggressive around a roadrunner and succeed in chasing it away. (I must confess there is something humorous in seeing a plump, seed-eating quail attacking a robust predator like the roadrunner.)

Birds of all kinds, particularly nestlings, make up about 2% of the roadrunner's diet. Adult birds are not generally taken as they are too large to be swallowed whole. There are, however, exceptions. Hummingbirds had been known to be captured in midair (Spofford, 1976) and a few years ago I received a reliable report of a roadrunner that had snagged a low-flying mockingbird. As is typical with large prey, the roadrunner held the mockingbird in its beak and began slamming it against the ground until it was dead. In this case, however, the whiplike snapping of the prey continued until both wings, both legs and many of the feathers had been shaken loose from the body. The mockingbird torso was then swallowed.

In a similar vein, I once observed a roadrunner that had found a tarantula. It grabbed the spider by a leg and slammed it against the ground. The action pulled the leg off but the spider was still able to walk and attempted to escape. The roadrunner quickly bit a second leg of the tarantula. Again the victim was slammed against the ground removing yet another leg. This gruesome scene was repeated until all the legs were gone. The spider was then swallowed.

Roadrunners don't have sharp and powerful tearing beaks as do hawks and falcons. The mockingbird and tarantula notwithstanding, most prey must be swallowed whole. This fact would severely limit the size of prey that can be eaten by roadrunners were it not for two behaviors: prey beating and incremental swallowing.

The function of prey beating was first described in 1979 in a research paper written by Kathleen Beal and Linda Gillam. Using x-rays, they demonstrated that multiple fractures were inflicted on a victim when it was held between a roadrunner's mandibles and repeatedly slammed against the ground. The fractures resulted in the prey having fewer lateral protrusions and greater malleability. In other words, the prey became easier to swallow.

It is not uncommon to observe a roadrunner with part of the last meal dangling from its mouth. This is particularly true with lizards

30

A roadrunner has captured a sidewinder, Crotalus cerastes.

A roadrunner attacks a snake in Red Rock Canyon State Park.

and snakes, the larger prey of roadrunners. After killing, or paralyzing as a result of multiple fractures of the vertebral column, snakes and large lizards are swallowed in increments. The roadrunner can, up to a point, accommodate a long victim by forcing it into a spiral in its stomach. But if the lizard or snake is too long the stomach becomes filled and the roadrunner is left with the back half of the victim hanging out of its mouth.

Many predators might avoid a long prey item or disgorge it when they realize that they have bitten off more they can chew, so to speak, but not the roadrunner! With a reptile dangling from its mouth, it simply finds a quiet place to rest and begins to digest its meal. Every few minutes it swallows another inch of the reptile as portions of the meal are passed further down the digestive tract. Sometimes it may take up to three hours before the tip of the reptile's tail disappears down the gullet of the roadrunner. Like prey beating, incremental swallowing allows roadrunners to consume larger prey than could otherwise be accommodated.

Roadrunners consume a wide variety of animals that are considered noxious to humans. Foremost on the list are insects which, taken as a group, are the dietary mainstay of adult roadrunners. Grasshoppers and crickets top the list, accounting for about a third of all food. One roadrunner was known to have crammed sixty-three grasshoppers into its digestive tract in one day. Cockroaches and snails are also consumed as are black widows and scorpions.

The roadrunner's most notorious victims are venomous snakes. I once observed a roadrunner in Saguaro National Park that had captured a western coral snake, *Micruroides euryxanthus*. This species is in the same family as the cobra and has very toxic venom. Allegedly its bright red, yellow and black rings serve to warn predators that tangling with it may prove lethal. This did not seem to dissuade the roadrunner that banged the coral snake repeatedly against the ground until it was lifeless, then quickly devoured it.

A roadrunner also does not hesitate in attacking a rattlesnake, as long as the snake is not too big. I have witnessed roadrunners quickly dispatch newborn rattlesnakes and approach, but not attack, rattlers over three feet in length. My best guess is that a rattler must be something less than eighteen inches for it to be attacked and consumed by the "snake killer." It seems the large girth and weight of a rattlesnake beyond that length preclude a roadrunner from making a meal of it.

This roadrunner has just dropped, but will soon eat, a tarantula.

The battle between a roadrunner and a rattlesnake is fascinating to observe and may last fifteen minutes. A roadrunner approaches a meal-sized rattlesnake cautiously at first, and then very aggressively as the fight ensues. The roadrunner's attack focuses on the rattler's head which it attempts to grab as the snake strikes. The roadrunner waves its tail from side to side and flares out its wings to distract the rattlesnake from more vulnerable parts of its body. Then, using its beak and feet to poke at the rattlesnake, it attempts to illicit a strike. Usually the rattler obliges and the roadrunner attempts to grab the head in midair. If successful, the rattler is doomed. Securing this hold, the roadrunner slams the snake over and over against the ground breaking its vertebral column, sometimes in more than a dozen places. The dead or paralyzed snake is then engulfed.

I have observed a rattler, around fifteen inches in length, avoid predation by hiding its head beneath its coils. Since the roadrunner is unlikely to persist in an attack if the rattler's head cannot be grabbed, this strategy works well. Without a head hold, the snake cannot be controlled and the roadrunner risks being bitten. (There is no reason to believe that roadrunners are immune to a rattler's venom and a bite would undoubtedly be lethal.)

With the arrival of winter the roadrunner's normal prey species become scarce. Lizards and snakes enter hibernation. Many insects die. Nestling birds have matured and many have flown south. Animal food is simply much more difficult to find. Roadrunners partially adapt to this food scarcity by relying more upon plant seeds and fruits in winter. Berries from *Rhus* shrubs, and seeds of *Atriplex* and cacti are some of the plant foods consumed. In total, plant materials make up about 10% of the roadrunner's diet each year.

The search for food during winter may cause roadrunners to change their daily foraging patterns. This might explain their disappearance from some areas. Further disappearances may be explained by roadrunner deaths. Many inexperienced young birds, and perhaps older birds as well, are likely to perish during this season of food scarcity and cold weather conditions. But there is one other possible explanation for their disappearance. Some roadrunners might be tucked away in the shelter of a dense shrub or rock crevice, in a deep, metabolic sleep.

A roadrunner leaps into the air to avoid a rattlesnake strike. The tail is thrust down to help lift it into the air.

A roadrunner watches a Cooper's Hawk fly overhead.

Dealing with Predators

Although roadrunners may be formidable predators, occasionally the tables are turned and the predator becomes the prey. This was dramatically revealed to me one morning while observing a family of roadrunners—a male, female, and their two offspring that had recently left the nest. The young roadrunners confined their activity to the vicinity of several large desert willow and palo verde trees while the parents were off on brief foraging trips to capture insects and lizards.

One of the young roadrunners had the habit of jumping up into a dead tree where it would perch for minutes at a time, presumably in the hope of being the first to see a parent return with food. The habit did not last long. One morning a Cooper's hawk (*Accipiter cooperii*) flew down the wash with great speed, striking the young roadrunner from behind. The youngster fell to the ground in a quivering pile. The hawk made a short loop in the air, then returned to pounce on its victim a final time.

That was not the last time I observed the Cooper's hawk hunting members of this roadrunner family. In fact, the hawk made a morning ritual of flying low over the wash where the roadrunners lived, apparently hoping to capture the other youngster unawares. But try as it might this never happened. The remaining youngster immediately ran for cover when any bird flew overhead and the adult roadrunners were far too wary to be taken by surprise.

Curiously, in this particular roadrunner family the adult male was quite confident in his ability to evade the attacking Cooper's hawk. On more than one occasion he would actually taunt the hawk and elicit an attack.

The most dramatic incident occurred on a very warm morning in early July. I had been observing the coming and going of the roadrunner pair since just after dawn. They had been out foraging and had returned to the center of their territory. Suddenly the

Cooper's hawk flew out of nowhere and dove at the pair. Both dashed for the cover of a palo verde tree and hid in its tangle of branches. The hawk flew up to the top of the tree and perched, but only for a few seconds. It then began flying around and around the tree causing the roadrunners to move from one side of the palo verde to the other but never to emerge from the protection of the branches.

After the hawk perched again atop the tree, the male roadrunner dashed across the wash and hid beneath another palo verde. The hawk immediately flew over to the new tree and once again circled. This time the roadrunner ran from beneath the branches and allowed the hawk to fly after it at least eight times around the tree.

At no point did the hawk come close to making a capture as the roadrunner was always able to stay out in front of its increasingly frustrated adversary. As a final strategy, the hawk flew to the ground and ran after the roadrunner. This was total folly for the hawk as it was less agile on the ground. Two chases around the tree was all it had left. Mouth agape and breathing laboriously, the exhausted Cooper's hawk flew to the top of the tree.

The roadrunner, on the other hand, seemed in high spirits and began taunting the bird of prey by running towards it and then running away. The roadrunner seemed to want to be chased. The hawk obliged one more time: first by running around the tree after the roadrunner and then by flying around the tree twice more. The roadrunner allowed the hawk to get closer this time but always remained just out of reach. The hawk landed once more on the ground staring at the roadrunner who stood not more than eight feet from it on open ground (see photograph on opposite page).

The hawk had met its match. Surprise was its best strategy and once the roadrunner was aware of its presence no amount of persistence was enough. The hawk slowly took to the air and flew down the wash away from the roadrunner.

The roadrunner, however, was not quite done. He immediately set out after the hawk, chasing it more than fifty yards down the wash until both birds finally disappeared around a bend.

Although I never again saw the roadrunner and the hawk play such an amazing game of cat and mouse, the hawk would swoop down upon the roadrunners several times each week sending them scurrying beneath palo verde trees. Both parents kept a watchful eye towards the sky at all times. Turkey vultures also frightened them and kept them under cover for a least a few minutes. Ravens and doves, however, were carefully observed at first appearance overhead but quickly dismissed.

Avian predators are undoubtedly the most significant enemies of roadrunners with Cooper's hawks and prairie falcons (*Falco mexicanus*) heading the list. There is also one record of a red-tailed hawk (*Buteo jamaicensis*) collected in 1935 that was discovered to have roadrunner remains in its stomach (Sutton, 1940).

Unlike hawks and falcons, terrestrial predators are not considered an important factor in roadrunner mortality. Indeed, there are no records of a bobcat, fox or coyote capturing an adult roadrunner. (This fact may disappoint *Roadrunner* cartoon aficionados who have witnessed *Wile E. Coyote* attempt to catch a roadrunner.)

Cooper's Hawk on ground during roadrunner attack.

This is not to say that terrestrial predators do not try to capture roadrunners. They clearly do as indicated by the unusual but highly predictable behavior of a roadrunner with eggs or young. When a terrestrial intruder approaches a roadrunner parent on its nest, the parent bird immediately jumps to the ground and attempts to lure the intruder away. Not by feigning a broken wing as would be done by some birds. But rather by feigning a broken leg! Hopping off the nest, the roadrunner collapses its body to the ground and wiggles rapidly from side to side. It continues this behavior while simultaneously shuffling over the ground in a direction away from the nest. To a human observer it appears that the roadrunner can hardly walk, let alone run. At fifty to one hundred feet from the nest, the parent bird suddenly stands erect and runs off at full speed–leaving the bewildered intruder behind.

As one might expect, it is roadrunner eggs and hatchlings that are most vulnerable to predation. Snakes are likely nest predators because of their ability to climb arborescent cacti and other armed plants. Both the common whipsnake (*Masticophis flagellum*) and bullsnake (*Pituophis melanoleucus*) feed on bird eggs and hatchlings and are found throughout the range of the roadrunner. However, no one has ever actually observed snake predation. Robert Ohmart (1973) found that nest predation was low or nonexistent on his roadrunner study sites near Tucson, Arizona.

Without question, humans are the greatest threat to roadrunners. Cars, domestic cat predation, and illegal hunting account for more adult roadrunner mortality than all other factors combined.

An alert Greater Roadrunner patrols its territory in Anza-Borrego Desert State Park.

Dealing With Extremes

The greatest portion of the roadrunner's range is desert, an environment known for prolonged drought, blistering summer temperatures, and often very cold winter nights. It is a land of extremes that often tests the physical and behavioral capacities of its inhabitants, including the roadrunner.

Acquiring sufficient water is one of the greatest challenges facing desert animals. For many animals, behavioral adjustments such as seeking shade or shelter, are usually sufficient in dealing with the daily extremes in temperature. But for all animals, even mild dehydration must be alleviated within twenty-four hours.

The roadrunner is basically a carnivore and thus feeds on other animals. Since the bulk of any animal's weight is water the roadrunner can obtain all the water it needs through its food. Put another way, as long as it finds enough animals to eat, its water requirements are satisfied.

Obtaining water, however, is only half the story. Conserving water can be equally important.

The roadrunner is a daytime-active predator. Unlike the coyote that becomes a nocturnal hunter during hot weather, the roadrunner cannot see well enough in dim light to hunt at night. It must therefore forage during daylight hours, even in summer. The roadrunner is also a strictly terrestrial predator and the desert's ground temperatures can approach 200 degrees Fahrenheit during the summer months. In short, a summer foraging roadrunner is often faced with being active when the air is hot and the ground blistering.

The potential danger of being diurnal and terrestrial in summer is overheating. Fortunately, the roadrunner can use evaporative cooling, as can humans, to prevent this. Although some evaporative cooling occurs on the roadrunner's skin, most occurs through a

Standing in the shade, mouth agape, wings
drooped and held away from its body, all
indicate a hot roadrunner trying to keep cool.

process that looks like a dog's panting but is correctly referred to as gular fluttering. By rapidly moving the skin of its throat, it forces air over the moist tissues of its breathing surfaces and accomplishes what humans do by sweating. The water from moist tissues in the mouth, throat and lungs evaporates rapidly in the dry desert air. The evaporating water cools the blood in these tissues and the relatively cool blood is then pumped throughout the body during normal circulation. So effective is this technique that a roadrunner, along with most other desert birds, can prevent its body from overheating even on the hottest days.

There is a cost to evaporative cooling, however. The practice uses the precious water supply in an animal's body—a supply that can be difficult to replace in a desert environment. For the roadrunner, eating moist food is just part of the solution to keeping cool and staying in water balance.

There are two additional strategies that must be used by the roadrunner as well as many other desert carnivores to deal with heat and aridity. They can (1) cut down on the amount of water lost through evaporative cooling or (2) find a source of drinking water. I have often seen roadrunners drink at desert streams, springs, and potholes. Their surprising abundance around the margins of urban areas no doubt partially reflects the availability of water. But I have also, albeit less frequently, observed roadrunners miles and miles from the nearest source of drinking water.

The roadrunner, as well as most other birds, possesses an important physiological trait that enables it to cut down on the amount of water lost through evaporative cooling—a naturally high body temperature. The normal operating temperature for a roadrunner during daylight hours is 104 degrees Fahrenheit. That's more than five degrees hotter than a human's normal operating temperature. With an adjustment for body size differences, this translates into significant water savings. Whereas the average human begins to perspire when the air temperature reaches just 80 degrees, the roadrunner does not gular flutter until the temperature is 97 degrees.

A roadrunner fluffs out its feathers to keep warm on a cool morning.

A roadrunner standing beside a human in the shade of a desert tree won't begin to actively use evaporative cooling until about two hours after the human has begun to perspire. The human will also be sweating for more than two hours after the roadrunner has stopped gular fluttering sometime in the late afternoon. In short, the high body temperature of the roadrunner cuts down on the need for evaporative cooling and conserves precious moisture.

Even with its high body temperature, a roadrunner without access to drinking water must still rely upon water conservation strategies. The most obvious one is to seek shade whenever possible. This is exactly what roadrunners do on hot days—spend a lot of time standing in the shade. Over the course of two summers, I watched a pair of roadrunners almost every day. I first observed them shortly after the sun rose above the horizon. Hunting began about an hour after sunrise and lasted for about three hours. As midday approached they retreated into the shade and rarely exposed themselves to the sun for any duration until mid-to-late afternoon. At the hottest time of day in midsummer, each roadrunner could be seen standing in the shade of a desert willow tree, mouth agape, throat rapidly flapping, and wings drooped down and away from the body. It got very hot and, frankly, the birds looked stressed. Even though they were probably hungry, they would not leave their shady retreat even for the live crickets I threw them. By late afternoon, however, they began foraging once more, finally retiring for the night about an hour before sunset.

The Greater Roadrunner demonstrates its most unusual adaptation at night while sleeping. I first noticed this trait while rearing a hatchling roadrunner at my home. After three weeks of gobbling down mealworms, crickets, and small mice, my roadrunner was ready to leave its makeshift shoe box nest. It was given the run of the yard for an hour each morning, placed in a flight enclosure during the day, and let out again each afternoon. At dusk it would voluntarily come into the house, enter my office, and jump onto my shoulder while I worked at the desk. There the young roadrunner would fall asleep snuggled as tightly as it could get against my head. After ten or fifteen minutes, I would lift the bird from my shoulder and place it in the shoe box on a shelf. During the transfer the bird never awakened, and no noise or flickering of room lights could arouse it. While all this was happening, I ran across a research paper written in 1971 by Robert Ohmart of Arizona State University. Ohmart's work indicated that his captive roadrunners allowed their body temperatures to drop ten degrees at night, from around 103 to 93 degrees Fahrenheit. Later, in 1982, Sandra Vehrencamp, presently with the Cornell Laboratory of Ornithology, confirmed that wild, free-ranging roadrunners also allowed their body temperature to drop significantly at night. With a lowered body temperature, and consequent reduced metabolism, it was no wonder that my hand-reared roadrunner slept so deeply. It was in nocturnal hypothermia, a kind of torpor that prevented it from responding even to my voice.

The advantage of nocturnal hypothermia for a wild roadrunner is simple: a lowered body temperature means the roadrunner saves energy at night and requires at least one less lizard per day as a result. Such an energy savings can be important, particularly during winter when most insects and reptiles are not available.

There are also, however, disadvantages to nocturnal hypothermia. One is that the roadrunner is very lethargic and unable to effectively run or fly. At night it would be easy prey for a predator and so must find an especially safe retreat where foxes and large owls cannot find it. As mentioned previously, dense shrubs and trees are often unavailable over the broad expanse of the desert Southwest. Without safe retreats, the roadrunner cannot occupy habitat that might otherwise be suitable.

A second disadvantage of nocturnal hypothermia is the large amount of energy needed to warm back up again each morning. It takes more energy to rewarm to 103 degrees F. than simply to maintain that temperature over the same period of time. This is where the roadrunner shows a remarkable adaptation. Shortly after dawn the roadrunner jumps down from its perch and immediately turns its backside to the sun. The wings are allowed to droop and the large feathers on its back are erected, exposing the unusual black skin

A roadrunner warms its body temperature by basking in the morning sun.

and small black feathers on its back. For many minutes, and sometimes intermittently for more than an hour, the roadrunner basks in this manner.

The net result of the behavior is a substantial energy savings since each basking roadrunner is using the sun's energy, not just food energy, to warm up each morning. The black skin and feathers facilitate this warming since black absorbs substantially more radiant energy than do other colors. In effect, the roadrunner is partially **solar-powered** not just in the morning but off and on throughout the day. This is particularly critical during the winter months.

The energy savings means the roadrunner can get by with a few less insects or one less lizard over the course of a day. Through the winter months, when food is particularly scarce, this energy savings can mean the difference between life and death for a roadrunner.

The roadrunner has binocular vision and
can see prey directly in front of its beak.
Carlsbad Caverns National Park

A nest and egg clutch of a Greater Roadrunner, Anza-Borrego Desert State Park.

Ensuring Descendents

Spring is normally the season when courtship begins. The breeding cycle is detected by humans when a male roadrunner finds the highest available perch and adds a mournful "oo, oo, ooo" to his normal bill-clattering repertoire. The "oooing" call is repeated several times and serves to dissuade other male roadrunners from entering the caller's territory and also to attract a mate. Once the breeding season is underway the call is made less often and not at all once young roadrunners have hatched.

Though conspicuous because of their relatively large size, roadrunners must be considered uncommon and not nearly as abundant as doves or finches. This situation reflects the fact that roadrunners are carnivores and predators and occupy a place near the top of the food chain. Life at the top may be less dangerous because of fewer potential predators, but it also means that there is a much smaller food base on which to draw. All this translates into fewer roadrunners when compared with seed-eating birds. This may very well be the reason that when a roadrunner finally finds a mate, the mate is kept for life.

Regardless of how attractive a female roadrunner may be to the male, it is she, not he, that does the choosing. After all, it is the female who must create the eggs, be hampered by their weight as they develop within her, and eventually extrude them into the nest. This is no small feat and requires an enormous cost in energy. If the female is going to run the risk of reproduction, she must find a mate who is fit, is an excellent provider, and is aggressive enough to ward off any other roadrunner that might threaten the couple's territory. Perhaps most importantly, she needs his help in providing the tremendous amount of food required by the developing young.

How does a female know which male will make a good mate and a reliable father? It appears that she relies on two behavior categories to provide the information she needs to make her decision. The

Greater Roadrunners mating - male holding food offering. Photograph by Jeff Foote.

first is the initial courtship. Amorous male roadrunners must proceed through a number of behavioral rituals that include lowering their head to the ground then raising it to the sky—a movement referred to as *sky pointing*. The tail is then moved back and forth—somewhat reminiscent of a dog wagging its tail. These behaviors are done intermittently during the initial courtship period. The male initiates courtship signals and the female mirrors the same movements. The ability of the male to properly perform these behaviors indicates that he is both physically and genetically fit.

The second male behavior scrutinized by the female involves a gift of food. Shortly after sizing each other up, the male offers a twig or other piece of nest-building material. He may drop this at her feet and she may pick it up in her beak. This kind of offering is preliminary to serious offerings. Serious offerings consist of food but not just any food. Serious offerings must be vertebrate animals such as lizards, snakes, small birds, or small rodents. Only when a serious offering is presented will the female finally consent to mating.

I suspect the offering of a vertebrate animal indicates to the female that her potential mate is fully capable of bringing in the kind of food that assures proper development of the young. Although adult roadrunners can survive on a diet of arthropods such as spiders and grasshoppers, young roadrunners will not develop properly on such a diet. Hatchling roadrunners reared in captivity on insects usually die, or, if they do survive, develop bone or other deformities. Hatchlings must be given mice or carefully prepared diets with the amino acids and minerals required by growing roadrunners. Thus, when an adult female selects a male with proper hunting abilities, she maximizes her chances of raising a healthy brood.

Copulation is repeated many times during early courtship. Actual mating begins by the male approaching the female with prey in his beak. He then jumps precariously onto her back. He turns his tail under hers, their cloacal openings meet, and he forces seminal fluid into her by contracting muscles surrounding his cloaca. The process is over in seconds and ends when the female turns her head upward and grabs the food from her mate's beak. Interestingly, the male never allows the female to take the prey until after mating.

The male's habit of offering prey to induce mating continues through the breeding season. The ritual, however, gets a bit casual as the

A young roadrunner peaks out from beneath its parent.

second round of breeding begins. By the second or third breeding phase, the male may refuse to give up the food prize after mating. The male dismounts and runs off to consume the lizard or snake himself. The female may protest with a brief chase, but does not succeed in getting the prize once the male decides to keep it.

If winter precipitation is above average, breeding and egg-laying may begin as early as January (Cornett, 1983). In those parts of the Southwest that typically receive summer rain, the breeding cycle may last from spring through early fall with several, successive clutches of eggs laid (Ohmart, 1973; Folse and Arnold, 1978). In California where summer rain is rare, roadrunners breed only from late winter to late spring. They may, however, lay and raise two or even three broods during this time period.

Clutch size varies between three and six. Both sexes incubate the eggs but night incubation is the exclusive domain of the male. At an extra cost in energy, he maintains a high body temperature for this purpose. Sandra Vehrencamp (1982) discovered that this behavior allowed the female to recuperate after egg-laying by allowing her to return to the energy saving habit of nocturnal hypothermia.

Both parents are needed to provide food for the young. Even so, in my experience only two, occasionally three, and rarely four chicks are successfully reared. This is not because some eggs do not hatch. Most eggs do hatch but they do so *asynchronously*. The female may take a week to lay an entire clutch but incubation begins when the first egg is laid. The result is that hatching is spread over several days and nestling roadrunners are of varying sizes. Inevitably, the last to hatch and smallest of the brood does not receive adequate food and is devoured by the parents or fed to a larger sibling. This may sound abhorrent, but the meal provided by a dying sibling may ensure the survival of another nestmate.

The availability of food resources in the arid Southwest can be erratic and depends largely upon the weather. In dry years, there may be too few prey animals to keep even one hatchling alive and the adults may skip breeding entirely. In wet years, roadrunners adapt by having larger clutches, raising more young successfully, and producing two, three or even four broods.

The first to hatch is the one most likely to fledge.

*Roadrunner petroglyph discovered by Lew Kingman in the
McCoy Mountains of California's Colorado Desert.*

Indians and Roadrunners

Every Southwest Indian group knew the roadrunner. There was a special word for the roadrunner in each language or dialect and the bird was a recurring character in the stories, myths, and legends of nearly every tribe.

Gertrude Leivas, a Chemehuevi woman, related a story of the roadrunner and the meaning of her own tribe's name (in Trimble, 1993):

> When they saw the land full of mesquite beans,
> they rushed down into the valley like a roadrunner,
> and this is what Chemehuevi means: 'nose in the
> air like a roadrunner.'

The Pima of southern Arizona called the bird d'adai (pronounced t'ad ie) and told a story to explain how the roadrunner acquired the brilliant patch of orange skin behind its eye (Curtin, 1949).

> "A long time ago an old woman had a pet rattlesnake
> and when it died she had no fire with which to cremate
> her pet. The roadrunner, offering to procure some for her,
> flew up to the sun, the journey taking four days. On his
> return trip, a thunderstorm arose and lightning struck
> him right on the head, but he brought the fire. That is
> how the roadrunner got red on his head."

The Paiute of southern Nevada called the roadrunner *soonung'wuvee toowuv* which means son of the coyote. They tell a story of how fire was stolen from another tribe and, in doing so, explain why the roadrunner has an odd arrangement of toes—two pointing to the front and two pointing to the rear. (Most birds have three toes pointing forward and one pointing backward.)

"Finally, Coyote, Roadrunner, and Jackrabbit tried to bring the sparks by relaying them. The relay was prearranged. Coyote stole the sparks (from the Indians in Utah) and took off. When he got tired he gave the sparks to Roadrunner who was followed (by the Utah Indians) but escaped when he fooled his pursuers by breaking his foot up, and making his tracks look as if they were going both ways. Those (Utah Indians) followingRoadrunner gave up and returned home (Martineau, 1992)."

The Cahuilla Indians of the Sonoran Desert of southeastern California referred to the roadrunner as *puuis* (pronounced poosh) and the bird is often mentioned in the oral history of these people. Chief Francisco Patencio, a Cahuilla Indian who lived in Palm Springs, stated in reference to the rarity with which the roadrunner takes flight that *"the month that the roadrunner flies means certain things"* (it is a sign). More generally he told how all wildlife was observed by the Cahuilla and that rare behavior, such as the appearance of the roadrunner, always had meaning . . .

> *and the habits of many other birds and animals all meant something to . . . older people who studied the signs of the sun and the moon and the stars and the animals.*

Most birds would be consumed by Native Americans if they could be caught. The relative scarcity of the roadrunner due to its position near the top of the food chain, along with it being difficult to capture, may explain why early Indian informants rarely mentioned it as a food resource. It is interesting to note, however, that roadrunner remains have been found intermingled with artifacts from ancient Pleistocene Indian hunting camps.

A Roadrunner Kachina carving known to the Hopi as Hospoa. *Hopi Kachinas are supernatural entities, embodying the spirits of living things. Each carving is a likeness of a spiritual Kachina and helps to reinforce beliefs. The Roadrunner Kachina carving reminds the Hopi of the importance of speed and agility in hunting and fighting. From the collections of the San Diego Museum of Man.*

Roadrunner Vital Statistics

Total Length: 24 inches

Adult Weight:

Male 12 ounces

Female 11 ounces

Clutch Size: 3 to 6

Egg Size: 1.54" X 1.20"

Incubation Period 18 days

Weight at hatching: 0.7 ounces

Age at Fledging: about 21 days

Age at Maturity: < 1 year

Life-span: > 6 years

Numerical values are averages.

References

Bailey, F. M. 1928. *Birds of New Mexico.* New Mexico Department of Game and Fish, Albuquerque, New Mexico.

Beal, K. G. 1978. Year-round weather-dependent behavior of the roadrunner (*Geococcyx californianus*). Ph.D.. dissertation, Ohio State University, Columbus, Ohio.

Beal, K. G. and L. D. Gillam. 1979. On the function of prey beating by roadrunners. Condor 81:85-87.

Bryant, H. C. 1916. Habits and food of the roadrunner in California. University of California Publications in Zoology 17(5):21-58.

Calder, W. A. 1967. Breeding behavior of the roadrunner, *Geococcyx californianus.* Auk 84:597-598.

Calder, W. A. 1967. The diurnal activity of the roadrunner, *Geococcyx californianus.* Condor 70:84-85.

Calder, W. A. and K. Schmidt-Nielsen. 1967. Temperature regulation and evaporation in the pigeon and the roadrunner. American Journal of Physiology 213:889-893.

Cornett, J. W. 1983. Early nesting of the roadrunner, *Geococcyx californianus,* in California. American Birds 37(2):236.

Cornett, J. W. 1998. Does the greater roadrunner hibernate? San Bernardino County Museum Quarterly 45(1,2):103.

Cornett, J. W. 1999. Roadrunner attack on juvenile desert tortoise. San Bernardino County Museum Quarterly 46(2):57-58.

Cornett, J. W. 1999. The greater roadrunner. The Desert Protective Council, Educational Bulletin #99-3.

Cornett, J. W. 2000. Unusual foraging strategy by the greater roadrunner. Western Birds 31:61-62.

Curtin, L. S. M. 1949. *By the prophet of the earth.* University of Arizona Press, Tucson, Arizona.

Folse, L. J., Jr. and K. A. Arnold. 1978. Population ecology of roadrunners (*Geococcyx californianus*) in south Texas. Southwestern Naturalist 21:1-28.

Hughes, J. M. 1996. Greater roadrunner (*Geococcyx californianus*), in The Birds of North America no. 244, Academy Natural Sciences, Philadelphia.

James, D. A. and J. C. Neal. 1986. *Arkansas birds: their distribution and abundance.* University of Arkansas Press, Fayetteville, Arkansas.

Lasiewski, R. C., M. H. Bernstein and R. D. Ohmart. 1971. Cutaneous water loss in the roadrunner and the poor-will. Condor 73:470-472.

Lowery, G. H. J. 1974. *Louisiana birds.* Louisiana State University Press, Baton Rouge, Louisiana.

Martineau, L. 1992. *The Southern Paiutes.* KC Publications., Las Vegas, Nevada.

Muller, K. A. 1971. Physical and behavioral development of a roadrunner raised at the National Zoological Park. Wilson Bulletin 83:186-193.

Ohmart, R. D. 1973. Observations on the breeding adaptations of the roadrunner. Condor 75:140-149.

Ohmart, R. D. and R. C. Lasiewski. 1971. Roadrunner: energy conservation by hypothermia and absorption of sunlight. Science 172:67-69.

Ohmart, R. D., and T. E. Chapman. 1970. Water turnover in roadrunners under different environmental conditions. Auk 87:787-793.

Pemberton, J. R. 1916. Variation of the broken-wing stunt by a roadrunner. Condor 18:203.

Rand, A. L. 1941. Courtship of the roadrunner. Auk 58:57-59.

Robbins, M. B. and D. A. Easterla. 1992. *Birds of Missouri: their distribution and abundance.* University of Missouri Press, Columbia, Missouri.

Russell, S. M. and G. Monson. 1998. *The birds of Sonora.* University of Arizona Press, Tucson.

Rylander, M. K. 1972. Winter dormitory of the roadrunner, *Geococcyx californianus* in west Texas. Auk 89:896.

Sutton, G. M. 1940. *Geococcyx californianus* (Lesson), roadrunner. Pages 36-51 in *Life histories of North American cuckoos, goatsuckers, hummingbirds, and their allies* (A. C. Bent, editor). U. S. Nat. Museum Bulletin No. 176.

Sutton, G. M. 1973. Winter food of a central Oklahoma roadrunner. Bulletin of the Oklahoma Ornithological Society 5:30.

Thompson, M. C. and C. Ely. 1989. *Birds in Kansas, Volume 1.* University of Kansas Museum of Natural History, Lawrence, Kansas.

Trimble, S. T. 1993. *The people.* School American Research Press, Santa Fe, New Mexico.

Vehrencamp, S. L. 1982. Body temperatures of incubating versus non-incubating roadrunners. Condor 84:203-207.

Webster, C. M. 2000. Distribution, habitat, and nests of the greater roadrunners in urban and suburban environments. Master's thesis, School of Renewable Natural Resources, University of Arizona, Tucson, Arizona.

Whitson, M. A. 1975. Courtship behavior of the greater roadrunner. Living Bird 14:215-255.